The National Strategy for Maritime Security

September 2005

The safety and economic security of the United States depends upon the secure use of the world's oceans. Since the attacks of September 11, 2001, the Federal government has reviewed and strengthened all of its strategies to combat the evolving threat in the War on Terrorism. Various departments have each carried out maritime security strategies which have provided an effective layer of security since 2001. In December 2004, the President directed the Secretaries of the Department of Defense and Homeland Security to lead the Federal effort to develop a comprehensive National Strategy for Maritime Security, to better integrate and synchronize the existing Department-level strategies and ensure their effective and efficient implementation.

Maritime security is best achieved by blending public and private maritime security activities on a global scale into an integrated effort that addresses all maritime threats. The new National Strategy for Maritime Security aligns all Federal government maritime security programs and initiatives into a comprehensive and cohesive national effort involving appropriate Federal, State, local, and private sector entities.

In addition to this Strategy, the Departments have developed eight supporting plans to address the specific threats and challenges of the maritime environment. While the plans address different aspects of maritime security, they are mutually linked and reinforce each other. The supporting plans include:

- National Plan to Achieve Domain Awareness
- Global Maritime Intelligence Integration Plan
- Interim Maritime Operational Threat Response Plan
- International Outreach and Coordination Strategy
- Maritime Infrastructure Recovery Plan
- Maritime Transportation System Security Plan
- Maritime Commerce Security Plan
- Domestic Outreach Plan

Development of these plans was guided by the security principles outlined in this National Strategy for Maritime Security. These plans will be updated on a periodic basis in response to changes in the maritime threat, the world environment, and national security policies.

Together, the National Strategy for Maritime Security and its eight supporting plans present a comprehensive national effort to promote global economic stability and protect legitimate activities while preventing hostile or illegal acts within the maritime domain.

Table of Contents

Section I
Introduction – Maritime Security

"In this century, countries benefit from healthy, prosperous, confident partners. Weak and troubled nations export their ills -- problems like economic instability and illegal immigration and crime and terrorism. America and others … understand that healthy and prosperous nations export and import goods and services that help to stabilize regions and add security to every nation."

President George W. Bush
November 20, 2004

The safety and economic security of the United States depend in substantial part upon the secure use of the world's oceans. The United States has a vital national interest in maritime security. We must be prepared to stop terrorists and rogue states before they can threaten or use weapons of mass destruction or engage in other attacks against the United States and our allies and friends. Toward that end, the United States must take full advantage of strengthened alliances and other international cooperative arrangements, innovations in the use of law enforcement personnel and military forces, advances in technology, and strengthened intelligence collection, analysis, and dissemination.

Salt water covers more than two-thirds of the Earth's surface. These waters are a single, great ocean, an immense maritime domain[1] that affects life everywhere. Although its four principal geographical divisions – Atlantic, Arctic, Indian, and Pacific – have different names, this continuous body of water is the Earth's greatest defining geographic feature.

The oceans, much of which are global commons under no State's jurisdiction, offer all nations, even landlocked States, a network of sea-lanes or highways that is of enormous importance to their security and prosperity. They are likewise a source of food, mineral resources, and recreation, and they support commerce among nations. They also act as both a barrier to and a conduit for threats to the security of people everywhere. Like all other countries, the United States is highly dependent on the oceans for its security and the welfare of its people and economy.

In today's economy, the oceans have increased importance, allowing all countries to participate in the global marketplace. More than 80 percent of the world's trade travels by water and forges a global maritime link. About half the world's trade by value, and

---

[1] The maritime domain is defined as all areas and things of, on, under, relating to, adjacent to, or bordering on a sea, ocean, or other navigable waterway, including all maritime-related activities, infrastructure, people, cargo, and vessels and other conveyances. Note: The maritime domain for the United States includes the Great Lakes and all navigable inland waterways such as the Mississippi River and the Intra-Coastal Waterway.

90 percent of the general cargo, are transported in containers. Shipping is the heart of the global economy, but it is vulnerable to attack in two key areas. Spread across Asia, North America, and Europe are 30 megaports/cities that constitute the world's primary, interdependent trading web. Through a handful of international straits and canals pass 75 percent of the world's maritime trade and half its daily oil consumption. International commerce is at risk in the major trading hubs as well as at a handful of strategic chokepoints.

The infrastructure and systems that span the maritime domain, owned largely by the private sector, have increasingly become both targets of and potential conveyances for dangerous and illicit activities. Moreover, much of what occurs in the maritime domain with respect to vessel movements, activities, cargoes, intentions, or ownership is often difficult to discern. The oceans are increasingly threatened by illegal exploitation of living marine resources and increased competition over nonliving marine resources. Although the global economy continues to increase the value of the oceans' role as highways for commerce and providers of resources, technology and the forces of globalization have lessened their role as barriers. Thus, this continuous domain serves as a vast, ready, and largely unsecured medium for an array of threats by nations, terrorists, and criminals.

Defeating this array of threats to maritime security – including the threat or use of weapons of mass destruction (WMD)[2] – requires a common understanding and a joint effort for action on a global scale. Because the economic well-being of people in the United States and across the globe depends heavily upon the trade and commerce that traverses the oceans, maritime security must be a top priority. Maritime security is required to ensure freedom of the seas; facilitate freedom of navigation and commerce; advance prosperity and freedom; and protect the resources of the ocean. Nations have a common interest in achieving two complementary objectives: to facilitate the vibrant maritime commerce that underpins economic security, and to protect against ocean-related terrorist, hostile, criminal, and dangerous acts. Since all nations benefit from this collective security, all nations must share in the responsibility for maintaining maritime security by countering the threats in this domain.

A strong world economy enhances our national security by advancing prosperity and freedom in the rest of the world. Economic growth supported by free trade and free markets creates new jobs and higher incomes. It allows people to lift their lives out of poverty, spurs economic and legal reform, and the fight against corruption, and it reinforces the habits of liberty. We will promote economic growth and economic freedom beyond America's shores.

Ignite a New Era of Global Economic Growth through Free Markets and
Free Trade
Goal VI of the *National Security Strategy of the United States*

---

[2] The term "weapon of mass destruction" (WMD) is defined in 18 U.S. Code § 2332a(c) as including any destructive device as defined in [18 U.S. Code] section 921...; any weapon that is designed or intended to cause death or serious bodily injury through the release, dissemination, or impact of toxic or poisonous chemicals, or their precursors; any weapon involving a biological agent, toxin, or vector (as those terms are defined in [18 U.S. Code] section 178...); or any weapon that is designed to release radiation or radioactivity at a level dangerous to human life.

Section II
Threats to Maritime Security

"America, in this new century, again faces new threats. Instead of massed armies, we face stateless networks; we face killers who hide in our own cities. We must confront deadly technologies. To inflict great harm on our country, America's enemies need to be only right once. Our intelligence and law enforcement professionals in our government must be right every single time."

President George W. Bush
December 17, 2004

Complexity and ambiguity are hallmarks of today's security environment, especially in the maritime domain. In addition to the potential for major combat operations at sea, terrorism has significantly increased the nature of the nonmilitary, transnational, and asymmetric threats in the maritime domain that the United States and its allies and strategic partners must be prepared to counter. Unlike traditional military scenarios in which adversaries and theaters of action are clearly defined, these nonmilitary, transnational threats often demand more than purely military undertakings to be defeated.

Unprecedented advances in telecommunications and dramatic improvements in international commercial logistics have combined to increase both the range and effects of terrorist activities, providing the physical means to transcend even the most secure borders and to move rapidly across great distances. Adversaries that take advantage of such transnational capabilities have the potential to cause serious damage to global, political, and economic security. The maritime domain in particular presents not only a medium by which these threats can move, but offers a broad array of potential targets that fit the terrorists' operational objectives of achieving mass casualties and inflicting catastrophic economic harm. While the variety of actors threatening the maritime domain continues to grow in number and capability, they can be broadly grouped as nation-states, terrorists, and transnational criminals and pirates. Defeating the threat of the widely dispersed terrorist networks that present an immediate danger to U.S. national security interests at home and abroad remains our foremost objective.

Nation-State Threats

The prospect of major regional conflicts erupting, escalating, and drawing in major powers should not be discounted. Nonetheless, in the absence of inter-state conflict, individual state actions represent a more significant challenge to global security. Some states provide safe havens for criminals and terrorists, who use these countries as bases of operations to export illicit activities into the maritime domain and into other areas of the globe. The probability of a hostile state using a WMD is expected to increase during the next decade.[3] An alternative danger is that a foreign state will provide critical advanced

---

[3] <u>Mapping the Global Future</u>, National Intelligence Council, Washington, DC: December 2004.

conventional weaponry, WMD components, delivery systems and related materials, technologies, and weapons expertise to another rogue state or a terrorist organization that is willing to conduct WMD attacks. WMD issues are of the greatest concern since the maritime domain is the likely venue by which WMD will be brought into the United States.

Terrorist Threats

Non-state terrorist groups that exploit open borders challenge the sovereignty of nations and have an increasingly damaging effect on international affairs. With advanced telecommunications, they can coordinate their actions among dispersed cells while remaining in the shadows. Successful attacks in the maritime domain provide opportunities to cause significant disruption to regional and global economies. Today's terrorists are increasing their effectiveness and reach by establishing links with other like-minded organizations around the globe. Some terrorist groups have used shipping as a means of conveyance for positioning their agents, logistical support, and generating revenue. Terrorists have also taken advantage of criminal smuggling networks to circumvent border security measures.

Terrorists have indicated a strong desire to use WMD.[4] This prospect creates a more complex and perilous security situation, further aggravated by countries that are unable to account for or adequately secure their stockpiles of such weapons and associated materials. This circumstance, coupled with increased access to the technology needed to build and employ those weapons, increases the possibility that a terrorist attack involving WMD could occur. Similarly, bioterrorism appears particularly suited to use by smaller but sophisticated groups because this tactic is exceedingly difficult to detect in comparison to other mass-effects weapons.

Terrorists can also develop effective attack capabilities relatively quickly using a variety of platforms, including explosives-laden suicide boats[5] and light aircraft; merchant and cruise ships as kinetic weapons to ram another vessel, warship, port facility, or offshore platform; commercial vessels as launch platforms for missile attacks; underwater swimmers to infiltrate ports; and unmanned underwater explosive delivery vehicles. Mines are also an effective weapon because they are low-cost, readily available, easily deployed, difficult to counter, and require minimal training. Terrorists can also take advantage of a vessel's legitimate cargo, such as chemicals, petroleum, or liquefied natural gas, as the explosive component of an attack. Vessels can be used to transport powerful conventional explosives or WMD for detonation in a port or alongside an offshore facility.

---

[4] The *National Security Strategy of the United States of America*, p. 15.
[5] This maritime mode of terrorist attack has been established, tested, and repeated. The terrorist group al-Qaida in October 2000 successfully attacked *USS Cole* in Yemen with an explosives-laden suicide small boat and 2 years later attacked the French oil tanker *M/V Limburg*.

The U.S. economy and national security are fully dependent upon information technology and the information infrastructure.[6] Terrorists might attempt cyber attacks to disrupt critical information networks, or attempt to cause physical damage to information systems that are integral to the operation of marine transportation and commerce systems. Tools and methodologies for attacking information systems are becoming widely available, and the technical abilities and sophistication of terrorists groups bent on causing havoc or disruption is increasing.

> However, the nature and motivations of these new adversaries, their determination to obtain destructive powers hitherto available only to the world's strongest states, and the greater likelihood that they will use weapons of mass destruction against us, make today's security environment more complex and dangerous.
>
> Prevent Our Enemies from Threatening Us, Our Allies, and Our Friends
> with Weapons of Mass Destruction
> Goal V of the *National Security Strategy of the United States*

Transnational Criminal and Piracy Threats

The continued growth in legitimate international commerce in the maritime domain has been accompanied by growth in the use of the maritime domain for criminal purposes. The smuggling of people, drugs, weapons, and other contraband, as well as piracy and armed robbery against vessels, pose a threat to maritime security. Piracy and incidents of maritime crime tend to be concentrated in areas of heavy commercial maritime activity, especially where there is significant political and economic instability, or in regions with little or no maritime law enforcement capacity. Today's pirates and criminals are usually well organized and well equipped with advanced communications, weapons, and high-speed craft. The capabilities to board and commandeer large underway vessels – demonstrated in numerous piracy incidents – could also be employed to facilitate terrorist acts.

Just as the world's oceans are avenues for a nation's overseas commerce, they are also the highways for the import or export of illegal commodities. Maritime drug trafficking[7] generates vast amounts of money for international organized crime syndicates and terrorist organizations. Laundered through the international financial system, this money provides a huge source of virtually untraceable funds. These monetary assets can then be used to bribe government officials, bypass established financial controls, and fund additional illegal activities, including arms trafficking, migrant smuggling, and terrorist operations. Further, these activities can ensure a steady supply of weapons and cash for terrorist operatives, as well as the means for their clandestine movement.

---

[6] The *National Strategy to Secure Cyberspace* is part of our overall effort to protect the Nation. It is an implementing component of the *National Strategy for Homeland Security* and is complemented by a *National Strategy for the Physical Protection of Critical Infrastructures and Key Assets*.
[7] The *National Drug Control Strategy* outlines U.S. goals in this area.

Environmental Destruction

Intentional acts that result in environmental disasters can have far-reaching, negative effects on the economic viability and political stability of a region. Additionally, in recent years, competition for declining marine resources has resulted in a number of violent confrontations as some of the world's fishers resort to unlawful activity. These incidents underscore the high stakes for the entire world as diminishing resources, such as fish stocks, put increasing pressure on maritime nations to undertake more aggressive actions. These actions continue to have the potential to cause conflict and regional instability. Similarly, massive pollution of the oceans, whether caused by terrorists or individuals who undertake intentional acts in wanton disregard for the consequences, could result in significant damage to ecosystems and undermine the national and economic security of the nations that depend on them.

Illegal Seaborne Immigration

International migration is a long-standing issue that will remain a major challenge to regional stability, and it will be one of the most important factors affecting maritime security through the next 10 years. Transnational migration, spurred by a decline of social well-being or internal political unrest, has become common over the past decades. It will continue to drive the movement of many people, with the potential to upset regional stability because of the strain migrants and refugees place on fragile economies and political systems. In some countries the collapse of political and social order prompts maritime mass migrations, such as the ones the United States has experienced from Cuba and Haiti. The humanitarian and enforcement efforts entailed by the management of such migrations require a significant commitment of security resources.

The potential for terrorists to take advantage of human smuggling networks in attempts to circumvent border security measures cannot be ignored. As security in our ports of entry, at land-border crossings, and at airports continues to tighten, criminals and terrorists will likely consider our relatively undefended coastlines to be less risky alternatives for unlawful entry into the United States.

Section III
Strategic Objectives

"It is the policy of the United States to take all necessary and appropriate actions, consistent with U.S. law, treaties and other international agreements to which the United States is a party, and customary international law as determined for the United States by the President, to enhance the security of and protect U.S. interests in the Maritime Domain..."

Presidential Directive
Maritime Security Policy
December 21, 2004

Today's transnational threats have the potential to inflict great harm on many nations. Thus, the security of the maritime domain requires comprehensive and cohesive efforts among the United States and many cooperating nations to protect the common interest in global maritime security. This Strategy describes how the United States Government will promote an international maritime security effort that will effectively and efficiently enhance the security of the maritime domain while preserving the freedom of the domain for legitimate pursuits. [8]

This approach does not negate the United States' inherent right to self-defense or its right to act to protect its essential national security interests. **Defending against enemies is the first and most fundamental commitment of the United States Government. Preeminent among our national security priorities is to take all necessary steps to prevent WMD from entering the country and to avert an attack on the homeland.** This course of action must be undertaken while respecting the constitutional principles upon which the United States was founded.

Three broad principles provide overarching guidance to this Strategy. First, *preserving the freedom of the seas* is a top national priority. The right of vessels to travel freely in international waters, engage in innocent and transit passage, and have access to ports is an essential element of national security. The free, continuing, unthreatened intercourse of nations is an essential global freedom and helps ensure the smooth operation of the world's economy.

Second, the United States Government must *facilitate and defend commerce* to ensure this uninterrupted flow of shipping. The United States is a major trading nation, and its economy, environment, and social fabric are inextricably linked with the oceans and their

---

[8] The *National Strategy for Maritime Security* is guided by the objectives and goals contained in the *National Security Strategy* and the *National Strategy for Homeland Security*. This Strategy also draws upon the *National Strategy for Combating Terrorism*, the *National Strategy to Combat Weapons of Mass Destruction*, the *National Strategy for the Physical Protection of Critical Infrastructure and Key Assets*, the *National Defense Strategy*, the *National Military Strategy*, and the *National Drug Control Strategy*.

resources. The adoption of a just-in-time delivery approach to shipping by most industries, rather than stockpiling or maintaining operating reserves of energy, raw materials, and key components, means that a disruption or slowing of the flow of almost any item can have widespread implications for the overall market, as well as upon the national economy.

Third, the United States Government must *facilitate the movement of desirable goods and people across our borders, while screening out dangerous people and material.* There need not be an inherent conflict between the demand for security and the need for facilitating the travel and trade essential to continued economic growth. This Strategy redefines our fundamental task as one of good border management rather than one that pits security against economic well-being. Accomplishing that goal is more manageable to the extent that screening can occur before goods and people arrive at our physical borders.

In keeping with these guiding principles, the deep-seated values enshrined in the U.S. Constitution, and applicable domestic and international law, the following objectives will guide the Nation's maritime security activities:

- Prevent Terrorist Attacks and Criminal or Hostile Acts
- Protect Maritime-Related Population Centers and Critical Infrastructures
- Minimize Damage and Expedite Recovery
- Safeguard the Ocean and Its Resources

This Strategy does not alter existing authorities or responsibilities of the department and agency heads, including their authorities to carry out operational activities or to provide or receive information. It does not impair or otherwise affect the authority of the Secretary of Defense over the Department of Defense, including the chain of command for military forces from the President and Commander-in-Chief, to the Secretary of Defense, to the commander of military forces, or military command and control procedures.

Prevent Terrorist Attacks and Criminal or Hostile Acts

Detect, deter, interdict, and defeat terrorist attacks, criminal acts, or hostile acts in the maritime domain, and prevent its unlawful exploitation for those purposes.

The United States will prevent potential adversaries from attacking the maritime domain or committing unlawful acts there by monitoring and patrolling its maritime borders, maritime approaches, and exclusive economic zones, as well as high seas areas of national interest, and by stopping such activities at any stage of development or deployment. The United States will work to detect adversaries before they strike; to deny them safe haven in which to operate unobstructed; to block their freedom of movement between locations; to stop them from entering the United States; to identify, disrupt, and dismantle their financial infrastructure; and to take decisive action to eliminate the threat they pose. As part of this undertaking, the *National Strategy to Combat Weapons of*

Mass Destruction and related presidential directives address the most serious of these threats, and outline plans and policies to execute timely, effective interdiction efforts against the proliferation of WMD, their delivery systems, and related materials, technologies, and expertise.

The basis for effective prevention[9] measures – operations and security programs – is awareness and threat knowledge, along with credible deterrent and interdiction capabilities. Without effective awareness of activities within the maritime domain, crucial opportunities for prevention or an early response can be lost. Awareness grants time and distance to detect, deter, interdict, and defeat adversaries – whether they are planning an operation, or are en route to attack or commit an unlawful act.

Forces must be trained, equipped, and prepared to detect, deter, interdict, and defeat terrorists throughout the maritime domain. Some terrorist groups, however, commit terrorist acts without regard to their own personal risk. They will never be easily deterred. No amount of credible deterrent capability can guarantee that attacks by such groups will be prevented. If terrorists cannot be deterred by the layered maritime security, then they must be interdicted and defeated, preferably overseas.

Protect Maritime-Related Population Centers and Critical Infrastructure

Protect maritime-related population centers, critical infrastructure, key resources, transportation systems, borders, harbors, ports, and coastal approaches in the maritime domain.

The United States depends on networks of critical infrastructure[10] – both physical networks such as the marine transportation system, and cyber networks such as interlinked computer operations systems. The ports, waterways, and shores of the maritime domain are lined with military facilities, nuclear power plants, locks, oil refineries, levees, passenger terminals, fuel tanks, pipelines, chemical plants, tunnels, cargo terminals, and bridges. Ports in particular have inherent security vulnerabilities: they are sprawling, easily accessible by water and land, close to crowded metropolitan areas, and interwoven with complex transportation networks. Port facilities, along with the ships and barges that transit port waterways, are especially vulnerable to tampering, theft, and unauthorized persons gaining entry to collect information and commit unlawful or hostile acts.

---

[9] The *National Response Plan* defines prevention as actions taken to avoid an incident or to intervene to stop an incident from occurring. It involves applying intelligence to a range of activities that may include such countermeasures as deterrence operations, improved security operations, and specific law enforcement operations aimed at deterring, preempting, interdicting, or disrupting illegal activity and apprehending potential perpetrators.

[10] The USA PATRIOT Act of 2001, 42 U.S.C. § 519 c(e), defines critical infrastructure as those "systems and assets, whether physical or virtual, so vital to the United States that the incapacity or destruction of such systems and assets would have a debilitating impact on security, national economic security, national public health or safety, or any combination of those matters."

The critical infrastructure and key resources of the maritime domain constitute a vital part of the complex systems necessary for public well-being, as well as economic and national security. They are essential for the free movement of passengers and goods throughout the world. Some physical and cyber assets, as well as associated infrastructure, also function as defense critical infrastructure, the availability of which must be constantly assured for national security operations worldwide. Beyond the immediate casualties, the consequences of an attack on one node of a critical infrastructure may include disruption of entire systems, significant damage to the economy, or the inability to project military forces. Protection of infrastructure networks must address individual elements, interconnecting systems, and their interdependencies.

Protection of critical infrastructure and key resources is a shared responsibility of the public and private sectors. The Department of Homeland Security is the lead agency for the overall national effort to enhance the protection of critical infrastructure and key resources. Since it is impossible to protect all infrastructure and resources constantly, all levels of government and the private sector must collectively improve their defenses by conducting prudent risk management assessments to identify facilities that require physical or procedural security upgrades or those that are not likely targets.

The Federal Government has three primary responsibilities in regard to this national effort: (1) to produce and distribute timely and accurate threat advisory and alert information and appropriate protective measures to State, local, and tribal governments and the private sector via a dedicated homeland security information network; (2) provide guidance and standards for reducing vulnerabilities; and (3) provide active, layered, and scalable security presence to protect from and deter attacks.

Since private industry owns and operates the vast majority of the nation's critical infrastructure and key resources, owners and operators remain the first line of defense for their own facilities. They are responsible for increasing physical security and reducing the vulnerabilities of their property by conducting routine risk management planning, as well as investing in protective measures – e.g., staff authentication and credentialing, access control, and physical security of their fixed sites and cargoes – as a necessary business function.

As security measures at ports of entry, land-border crossings, and airports become more robust, criminals and terrorists will increasingly consider the lengthy U.S. coastline with its miles of uninhabited areas as a less risky alternative for unlawful entry into the United States. The United States must therefore patrol, monitor, and exert unambiguous control over its maritime borders and maritime approaches. At-sea presence reassures U.S. citizens, deters adversaries and lawbreakers, provides better mobile surveillance coverage, adds to warning time, allows seizing the initiative to influence events at a distance, and facilitates the capability to surprise and engage adversaries well before they can cause harm to the United States.

Minimize Damage and Expedite Recovery

Minimize damage and expedite recovery from attacks within the maritime domain.

The United States must be prepared to minimize damage and expedite recovery[11] from a terrorist attack or other Incident of National Significance[12] that may occur in the maritime domain. Our experience dealing with the catastrophic effects of Hurricane Katrina reinforces this key point. The response to such incidents is implemented through the comprehensive National Incident Management System, governed by the *National Response Plan*, which coordinates public and private sector efforts and brings to bear all required assets, including defense support of civil authorities.

The public and private sectors must be ready to detect and rapidly identify WMD agents; react without endangering first responders; treat the injured; contain and minimize damage; rapidly reconstitute operations; and mitigate long-term hazards through effective decontamination measures. These actions will preserve life, property, the environment, and social, economic, and political structures, as well as restore order and essential services for those who live and work within the maritime domain.

A terrorist attack or similarly disruptive Incident of National Significance involving the marine transportation system can cause a severe ripple effect on other modes of transportation, as well as have adverse economic or national security effects. From the onset of a maritime incident, Federal, State, local, and tribal authorities require the capability to assess the human and economic consequences in affected areas rapidly, and to calculate the effects that may radiate outward to affect other regional, national, or global interests. These entities must also develop and implement contingency procedures to ensure continuity of operations, essential public services, and the resumption or redirection of maritime commercial activities, including the prioritized movement of cargoes to mitigate the larger economic, social, and possibly national security effects of the incident. Recovery of critical infrastructure, resumption of the marine transportation system, and restoration of communities within the affected area must all occur simultaneously and expeditiously.

---

[11] Recovery is defined by the *National Response Plan* as the development, coordination, and execution of service- and site-restoration plans for impacted communities and the reconstitution of government operations and services.

[12] An Incident of National Significance is based on the criteria established in Homeland Security Presidential Directive-5, Management of Domestic Incidents, February 2003.

Safeguard the Ocean and Its Resources

Safeguard the ocean and its resources from unlawful exploitation and intentional critical damage.

The unlawful or hostile exploitation of the maritime domain also requires attention. The vulnerability is not just within U.S. territorial seas and internal waters. In the future, the United States can anticipate increased foreign fishing vessel incursions into its exclusive economic zones, which may have serious economic consequences for the United States. Protecting our living marine resources from unlawful or hostile damage has become a matter of national concern. Potential consequences of such damage include conflict and regional instability among nations over the control of marine resources to the detriment of all. The United States and other nations have a substantial economic and security interest in preserving the health and productive capacity of the oceans. We will continue to project a U.S. presence by monitoring and patrolling the United States' exclusive economic zones and certain high seas areas of national interest.

Assisting regional partners to maintain the maritime sovereignty of their territorial seas and internal waters is a longstanding objective of the United States and contributes directly to the partners' economic development as well as their ability to combat unlawful or hostile exploitation by a variety of threats. For example, as a result of our active discussions with African partners, the United States is now appropriating funding for the implementation of border and coastal security initiatives along the lines of the former Africa Coastal Security (ACS) Program. Preventing unlawful or hostile exploitation of the maritime domain requires that nations collectively improve their capability to monitor activity throughout the domain, establish responsive decision-making architectures, enhance maritime interdiction capacity, develop effective policing protocols, and build intergovernmental cooperation. The United States, in cooperation with its allies, will lead an international effort to improve monitoring and enforcement capabilities through enhanced cooperation at the bilateral, regional, and global level.

Section IV
Strategic Actions

"The tasks of the 21ˢᵗ century ... cannot be accomplished by a single nation alone."

President George W. Bush
December 1, 2004

The United States recognizes that, because of the extensive global connectivity among businesses and governments, its maritime security policies affect other nations, and that significant local and regional incidents will have global effects. Success in securing the maritime domain will not come from the United States acting alone, but through a powerful coalition of nations maintaining a strong, united, international front. The need for a strong and effective coalition is reinforced by the fact that most of the maritime domain is under no single nation's sovereignty or jurisdiction. Additionally, increased economic interdependency and globalization, largely made possible by maritime shipping, underscores the need for a coordinated international approach. Less than 3 percent of the international waterborne trade of the United States is carried on vessels owned, operated, and crewed by U.S. citizens. The United States also recognizes that the vast majority of actors and activities within the maritime domain are legitimate. Security of the maritime domain can be accomplished only by seamlessly employing all instruments of national power in a fully coordinated manner in concert with other nation-states consistent with international law.

Maritime security is best achieved by blending public and private maritime security activities on a global scale into a comprehensive, integrated effort that addresses all maritime threats. Maritime security crosses disciplines, builds upon current and future efforts, and depends on scalable layers of security to prevent a single point of failure. Full and complete national and international coordination, cooperation, and intelligence and information sharing among public and private entities are required to protect and secure the maritime domain. Collectively, these five strategic actions achieve the objectives of this Strategy:

- Enhance International Cooperation
- Maximize Domain Awareness
- Embed Security into Commercial Practices
- Deploy Layered Security
- Assure Continuity of the Marine Transportation System

These five strategic actions are not stand-alone activities. Domain awareness is a critical enabler for all strategic actions. Deploying layered security addresses not only layers of prevention (interdiction and preemption) and protection (deterrence and defense) activities, but also the integration of domestic and international layers of security provided by the first three strategic actions.

Enhance International Cooperation

Enhance international cooperation to ensure lawful and timely enforcement actions against maritime threats.

As the world's individual national economies become ever more closely integrated, it is critical that nations coordinate and, where appropriate, collectively integrate their security activities to secure the maritime domain. Accordingly, the United States supports close cooperation among nations and international organizations that share common interests regarding the security of the maritime domain. This strategic action is designed to involve all nations that have an interest in maritime security, as well as the ability and willingness to take steps to defeat terrorism and maritime crime. Fundamental to this cooperation must be a shared understanding of threat priorities to unify actions and plans.

New initiatives are needed to ensure that all nations fulfill their responsibilities to prevent and respond to terrorist or criminal actions with timely and effective enforcement. More robust international mechanisms will ensure improved transparency in the registration of vessels and identification of ownership, cargoes, and crew of the world's multinational, multi-flag merchant marine. Weak regulations and enforcement by some nations hinder transparency. Terrorists and criminals are currently exploiting this vulnerability by re-registering vessels under fictitious corporate names, and renaming and repainting vessels. New initiatives will be pursued diplomatically through international organizations such as the International Maritime Organization, the World Customs Organization, and International Standards Organization that already involve strong participation by industry. Where appropriate, these initiatives will build upon existing efforts, such as the Container Security Initiative, the Proliferation Security Initiative, the Customs-Trade Partnership Against Terrorism, the nonproliferation amendments to the Convention for the Suppression of Unlawful Acts against the Safety of Maritime Navigation and the International Code for the Security of Ships and Port Facilities (ISPS Code), and the 2002 amendments to the International Convention for the Safety of Life at Sea, 1974. Initiatives will be coordinated by the Department of State and will include provisions such as:

- Implementing standardized international security and World Customs Organization frameworks for customs practices and standards to ensure that goods and people entering a country do not pose a threat;

- Expanding the use of modernized and automated systems, processes, and trade-data information to make vessel registration, ownership, and operation, as well as crew and cargo identification, more transparent and readily available in a timely manner;

- Developing, funding, and implementing effective measures for interdicting suspected terrorists or criminals;

- Developing and expanding means for rapid exchanges among governments of relevant intelligence and law enforcement information concerning suspected terrorist or criminal activity in the maritime domain;

- Adopting streamlined procedures to verify nationality and take appropriate and verifiable enforcement action against vessels in a timely manner consistent with the well-established doctrine of exclusive flag State jurisdiction;

- Expanding the United States Government's capabilities to prescreen international cargo prior to lading;

- Adopting procedures for enforcement action against vessels entering or leaving a nation's ports, internal waters, or territorial seas when they are reasonably suspected of carrying terrorists or criminals or supporting a terrorist or criminal endeavor; and

- Adopting streamlined procedures for inspecting vessels reasonably suspected of carrying suspicious cargo and seizing such cargo when it is identified as subject to confiscation.

The smooth operation of the global economy depends on the free flow of shipping through straits used for international navigation. About one third of the world's trade and half its oil traverse the Straits of Malacca and Singapore. Many of these key international waterways are relatively narrow and could be closed to shipping, at least temporarily, by an accident or terrorist attack. The United States will use the agencies and components of the Federal Government in innovative ways to improve the security of sea-lanes that pass through international straits. We will work with our regional and international partners to expand maritime security efforts. Regional maritime security regimes are a major international component of this Strategy and are essential for ensuring the effective security of regional seas.

The United States will continue to promote development of cooperative mechanisms for coordinating regional measures against maritime threats that span national boundaries and jurisdictions. By reducing the potential for regional conflict, maritime security is enhanced worldwide. The United States will also work closely with other governments and international and regional organizations to enhance the maritime security capabilities of other key nations by:

- Offering maritime and port security assistance, training, and consultation;

- Coordinating and prioritizing maritime security assistance and liaison within regions;

- Allocating economic assistance to developing nations for maritime security to enhance security and prosperity;

- Promoting implementation of the Convention for the Suppression of Unlawful Acts against the Safety of Maritime Navigation and its amendments and other international agreements; and

- Expanding the International Port Security and Maritime Liaison Officer Programs, and the number of agency attachés.

Maximize Domain Awareness

Maximize domain awareness to support effective decision-making.

A key national security requirement is the effective understanding of all activities, events, and trends within any relevant domain – air, land, sea, space, and cyberspace – that could threaten the safety, security, economy, or environment of the United States and its people. Awareness and threat knowledge are critical for securing the maritime domain and the key to preventing adverse events. Knowledge of an adversary's capabilities, intentions, methods, objectives, goals, ideology, and organizational structure, plus factors that influence his behavior, are used to assess adversary strengths, vulnerabilities, and centers of gravity. Such knowledge is essential to supporting decision-making for planning, identifying requirements, prioritizing resource allocation, and implementing maritime security operations. Domain awareness enables the early identification of potential threats and enhances appropriate responses, including interdiction at an optimal distance with capable prevention forces.

Achieving awareness of the maritime domain is challenging. The vastness of the oceans, the great length of shorelines, and the size of port areas provide both concealment and numerous access points to the land. Many maritime threats are conveyed in ways that thwart early detection and interdiction. The lack of complete transparency into the registration and ownership of vessels and cargoes, as well as the fluid nature of the crewing and operational activities of most vessels, offer additional opportunities for concealment and challenges for those attempting to maintain maritime security. Domain awareness requires integrating all-source intelligence, law enforcement information, and open-source data from the public and private sectors. It is heavily dependent on information sharing and requires unprecedented cooperation among the various elements of the public and private sectors, both nationally and internationally.

To maximize domain awareness, the United States will leverage its global maritime intelligence capability and the diverse expertise of the intelligence and law enforcement communities. The efforts of the existing maritime collection and analysis means will contribute to an intelligence enterprise equipped to collect, fuse, integrate, and disseminate timely intelligence and information. This intelligence enterprise will support United States Government agencies and international partners in securing the maritime domain, as well as their other statutorily assigned missions. Additionally, the Departments of Homeland Security, Defense, and Justice will oversee the implementation of a shared situational awareness capability that integrates intelligence, surveillance, reconnaissance, navigation systems, and other operational information inputs, combined with access at multiple levels throughout the United States Government. Authorized elements in the public and private sectors will have access to this integrated shared situational awareness capability, as well as relevant information within their specific area of responsibility. The establishment of this intelligence enterprise underscores the need for an integrated and robust maritime command and control system to defeat all maritime threats.

> "The increasing mobility and destructive potential of modern terrorism has required the United States to rethink and renovate fundamentally its systems for border and transportation security. Indeed, we must now begin to conceive of border security and transportation security as fully integrated requirements because our domestic transportation systems are inextricably intertwined with the global transport infrastructure. Virtually every community in America is connected to the global transportation network by the seaports, airports, highways, pipelines, railroads, and waterways that move people and goods into, within, and out of the Nation. We must therefore promote the efficient and reliable flow of people, goods, and services across borders, while preventing terrorists from using transportation conveyances or systems to deliver implements of destruction."
>
> *National Strategy for Homeland Security*

The United States will continue to enhance the capabilities of current systems and develop new capabilities and procedures to locate and track maritime threats and illicit activities. Initiatives to maximize domain awareness include expansion and enhancement of the following:

- Both short- and long-range vessel detection and monitoring capabilities;

- Regulatory and private sector initiatives and agreements to enhance advance notices of arrival, vessel movement information, supply-chain security practices, and manifest and entry information for cargo;

- International arrangements that promote enhanced visibility into the maritime supply chain and the movement of cargo, crews, and passengers;

- Sensor technology, human intelligence collection, and information processing tools to persistently monitor the maritime domain;

- International coalitions to share maritime situational awareness on a timely basis;

- Global maritime intelligence and integration enterprise for intelligence analysis, coordination, and integration that supports all other national efforts;

- Shared situational awareness to disseminate information to users at all levels;

- Automated tools to improve data fusion, analysis, and management in order to systematically track large quantities of data, and to detect, fuse, and analyze aberrant patterns of activity – consistent with the information privacy and other legal rights of Americans; and

- In order to advance to the next level of threat detection, transformational research and development programs in information fusion and analysis – these programs will develop the next qualitative level of capability for detection threats.

Embed Security into Commercial Practices

Embed security into commercial practices to reduce vulnerabilities and facilitate commerce.

Potential adversaries are opportunistic and will attempt to exploit existing vulnerabilities, choosing the time and place to act according to the weaknesses they observe. Private owners and operators of infrastructure, facilities, and resources are the first line of defense for their own property, and they should undertake basic facility security improvements. They can improve their defenses against terrorist attacks and criminal acts by embedding into their business practices scalable security measures that reduce systemic or physical vulnerabilities. The elimination of security weaknesses depends upon incorporating best practices and establishing centers of excellence, including feedback loops for lessons learned, as well as a periodic review of each country's security standards for mutual compatibility.

A close partnership between government and the private sector is essential to ensuring critical infrastructure and key resource vulnerabilities are identified and corrected quickly. Since 2001, the United States Government has developed and implemented a cargo container security strategy to identify, target, and inspect cargo containers before they reach U.S. ports. Under this strategy, the United States Government uses intelligence to review information on 100 percent of all cargo entering U.S. ports, and all cargo that presents a risk to our country is inspected using large x-ray and radiation detection equipment.

Additionally, the United States Government requires that advance information about all containers be given to U.S. Customs and Border Protection well before they arrive. In fact, the information is required 24 hours before cargo is loaded onto vessels at foreign seaports (24-Hour Rule). Containers posing a potential terrorist threat are identified and targeted before they arrive at U.S. seaports by the National Targeting Center (NTC). The NTC was established as the centralized coordination point for all of Customs and Border Protection's anti-terrorism efforts. NTC uses intelligence and terrorist indicators to review advance information for all cargo, passengers, and imported food shipments before arrival into the United States. NTC coordinates with other Federal agencies such as the U.S. Coast Guard, Federal Air Marshals, FBI, Transportation Security Administration, and the Departments of Energy and Agriculture, as well as the intelligence community.

Both the government and the private sector will continue to conduct vulnerability assessments to identify defenses that require improvement. A consistent risk management approach, which requires a comprehensive assessment of threat, likelihood, vulnerability, and criticality, will allow the private sector to invest in protective measures as a supporting business function.

Further reduction in security vulnerabilities will also occur by encouraging the private sector, by means of outcome-based security standards, incentives, and market mechanisms, to conduct comprehensive self-assessments of their supply chain security practices; adhere voluntarily to baseline security criteria; and implement other regulatory security measures as deemed necessary by the Department of Homeland Security. Enhanced reporting, verification, and compliance procedures by the private sector, as well as the use of technology to allow greater visibility into the supply chain, will enable the government to develop more accurate processes for separating high-risk cargo from that which can be afforded expedited clearance. In exchange, the shipments of firms that comply will be eligible for expedited clearance and have a reduced likelihood of inspections at departure, transshipment, and arrival ports.

The complexity of the process for handling containerized shipments makes it more difficult to embed security practices and reduce vulnerabilities than for other types of cargo. Container ships carry cargo for thousands of companies, and the containers are loaded individually away from the port. Each transfer of a container from one party to the next is a point of vulnerability in the supply chain. The security of each transfer facility and the trustworthiness of each company are therefore critical to the overall security of the shipment. Cargo must be loaded in containers at secure facilities and the integrity of the container maintained to its final destination. Supply chain personnel will employ various methods to prevent the misuse of containers and conveyances for transporting illegal commodities, as well as to detect tampering. They will report the occurrence of each incident to the Department of Homeland Security and, when appropriate, resolve such incidents prior to the arrival of the identified containers in the United States.

Embedding security practices and vulnerability reduction efforts into commercial practices rests upon the implementation of key legislation, such as the Maritime Transportation Security Act of 2002 and the Trade Act of 2002, as well as International Maritime Organization requirements such as the International Ship and Port Facility Security Code, and public-private partnerships such as the Customs-Trade Partnership Against Terrorism. The United States will build upon these statutes, international instruments, and identified best practices to develop a program of formal maritime security governance.

Commercial businesses must put in place effective means to control access to their facilities. In cooperation with the private sector, the United States will establish a system-wide common credential for use across all transportation modes by individuals requiring unescorted physical access to secure, restricted, and critical areas of the maritime domain. The identification card for access will use biometrics to link the person to the credential definitively. To receive this credential, individuals will undergo appropriate background checks. Credential services will also be available on a voluntary basis for frequent travelers under various registered traveler programs.

Overly restrictive, unnecessarily costly, or reactionary security measures to reduce vulnerabilities can result in long-term harm both to the United States and global economies, undermine positive countermeasures, and unintentionally foster an environment conducive to terrorism. Security measures must accommodate commercial and trade requirements, facilitate faster movement of more cargo and more people, and respect the information privacy and other legal rights of Americans. To support the accelerating growth of global commerce and security concerns, security measures must: (1) be aligned and embedded with supply chain information flows and business processes; (2) keep pace with supply chain developments; (3) optimize the use of existing databases; and (4) be implemented with the minimum essential impact on commercial and trade-flow costs and operations. This will require new and enhanced partnerships, as well as cost- and burden-sharing between the private and public sectors.

Deploy Layered Security

Deploy layered security to unify public and private security measures.

The ability to achieve maritime security is contingent upon a layered security system that integrates the capabilities of governments and commercial interests throughout the world. The public and private sectors acting in concert can prevent terrorist attacks and criminal acts only by using diverse and complementary measures, rather than relying upon a single point solution. Specifically, a layered approach to maritime security means applying some measure of security to each of the following points of vulnerability: transportation, staff, passengers, conveyances, access control, cargo and baggage, ports, and security *en route*. This layered security is not static, but deters attack by continually evolving through calculated improvements that introduce uncertainty into the adversary's deliberate planning process and efforts to conduct surveillance or reconnaissance. In deciding whether to implement a new security layer, the United States must take into account its effectiveness and cost in reducing risks Americans face, both in absolute terms and relative to other possible measures, and must ensure consistency with the information privacy and other legal rights of Americans.

- The Department of Homeland Security, the Department of Defense, and the Department of Justice, as well as the Department of State when diplomatic activities are required, will lead the United States' efforts to integrate and align all United States Government maritime security programs and initiatives into a comprehensive, cohesive national effort of scalable, layered security. This includes full alignment and coordination with appropriate State and local agencies, the private sector, and other nations.

- To intercept and defeat transnational threats, the Department of Homeland Security and the Department of Defense will develop a mutually agreed process for ensuring rapid, effective support to each other. Terrorist threats will be addressed as national security incidents employing as appropriate all instruments of national power to defeat the threat. All other maritime threats will be addressed through national authorities, consistent with national and international law, for mission accomplishment and self-defense, employing use-of-force protocols where necessary.

<u>Physical protection</u> is a fundamental layer of security. Primary protection measures by government agencies include maritime security or enforcement zones, vessel movement control, and the inspection of targeted cargo. Security zones are established and enforced around designated fixed facilities, certain vessels in transit, and sensitive geographic areas to provide an exclusion zone for controlled access and use only by the government. Around these zones, the private sector employs other layers of physical security, such as access barriers, fencing, lighting, surveillance cameras, and guards, along with oversight procedures, to ensure system integrity for the critical infrastructure and key resources that they own and operate. Security standards and procedures employed in the United States are developed in conjunction with other nations and industry, and are shared with State, local, and tribal governments.

- The rapid and accurate identification of individuals for access to secure, restricted, and critical areas is a paramount protection measure that must be implemented by the private sector, in cooperation with the Federal Government. Persons seeking to enter the United States will undergo identity checks and biometric screening at the border and in the coastal approaches to verify their lawful admission.

- Protection layers also include the positive control of high-interest vessels. Mandatory adherence to a national vessel-movement reporting system is required for all vessels entering and departing U.S. ports. Security forces assigned to provide physical security for critical infrastructure and key resources must be trained and equipped to detect, identify, interdict, and defeat vessels that pose a threat.

- Not all maritime assets, facilities, systems, or ports require equal protection. The Federal Government will collaborate with State, local, and tribal governments and the private sector to assess and prioritize critical facilities, resources, infrastructure, and venues that are at greatest risk from hostile or unlawful acts.

<u>Physical cargo inspection</u> adds another layer of security. With as many as 30,000 containers entering the United States every day, physical inspection of all cargo would effectively shut down the entire U.S. economy, with ripple effects far beyond the seaports. Inspections on this scale are prohibitively expensive and often ineffective. Using mandatory reporting information provided by the private sector, the United States will screen all inbound cargo and inspect all cargo designated as high-risk and ideally prescreen it before loading. In addition, all inbound cargo will be screened for WMD or their components. Establishment of the Domestic Nuclear Defense Office will contribute to improving the detection of a nuclear device or fissile or radiological material entering the United States through the maritime domain.

<u>Interdiction of personnel and materials</u> that pose a threat to the United States or the maritime domain is an essential layer of security. Interdiction, whether against terrorist personnel, terrorist materiel support, WMD, or other contraband, will be carefully coordinated to ensure prioritization of intelligence, proper allocation of resources, and, when necessary, swift, decisive action. The United States, along with its international partners, will monitor those vessels, cargoes, and people of interest from the point of

origin, through intervening ports, to the point of entry to ensure the integrity of the transit, to manage maritime traffic routing, and, if necessary, to interdict or divert vessels for inspection and search. The United States will promote efforts to enhance the efficiency and effectiveness of detecting and determining the status of unidentified or unauthorized vessels, people, and cargo within the maritime domain.

Military and law enforcement response provides a fourth security layer. For maritime security operations on the high seas or in its exclusive economic zones, territorial seas, internal seas, inland rivers, ports, and waterways, the United States must have well-trained, properly equipped, and ready maritime security forces from both the U.S. Armed Forces and national, regional, State, and local law enforcement agencies to detect, deter, interdict, and defeat any potential adversary. For protection and deterrence to be successful, maritime security forces must be visible, vigilant, well-trained, well-equipped, mobile, adaptive, and capable of generating effective presence quickly, randomly, and unpredictably.

In many instances each layer of maritime security is the responsibility of a different agency with multiple jurisdictions and functions. Integrating these disparate maritime security layers requires a clear delineation of roles and responsibilities and cannot be achieved through cooperation alone. In particular, to achieve unity of effort and operational effectiveness, maritime security forces from both the U.S. Armed Forces and law enforcement agencies must have the capability and authority to operate in mutually supporting and complementary roles against the spectrum of expected security threats. These security forces must have a high degree of interoperability, reinforced by joint, interagency, international training and exercises to ensure a high rate of readiness, and supported by compatible communications and, where appropriate, common doctrine and equipment.

- Recognizing the critical importance of interoperability, maritime security actions at the operational and tactical levels will be based on a network-centric approach that employs resources, as needed, from multiple agencies – primarily from the Department of Homeland Security and the Department of Defense – including surveillance and reconnaissance assets, aircraft, ships, boats, land units, and shore support facilities, all linked by an operational information network.

- Wherever feasible and operationally effective, agencies should co-locate in multiagency centers to facilitate direct interaction and efficient use of limited resources. Additionally, concrete and well-defined coordination protocols and communication mechanisms including procedures for operating jointly to prevent and respond to threats, and for assigning lead agencies for both pre- and post-incident operations, will be implemented. The coordination protocols must also outline defined procedures for ensuring national execution of maritime security policy for specific threats or incidents, and more routine encounters where a multiagency response must be seamlessly coordinated.

- Integrated planning and effective management of agency resources – Federal, State, and local – are essential for an effective response. Therefore, agencies will also share training, planning, and other resources, where practical and permissible, to standardize operational concepts, develop common technology requirements, and coordinate budget planning for maritime security missions.

- Acquisition and logistics processes must support the continuous assessment of all requirements to optimize the allocation of appropriate resources and capabilities. Cooperative research and development efforts, coupled with reformed acquisition processes with coordinated requirements, funding, and scheduling, along with management, will identify unmet and emerging needs.

Assure Continuity of the Marine Transportation System

Assure continuity of the marine transportation system to maintain vital commerce and defense readiness.

The United States will be prepared to maintain vital commerce and defense readiness in the aftermath of any terrorist attack or other similarly disruptive incidents that occur within the maritime domain. The response to such events should not default to an automatic shutdown of the marine transportation system; instead, the United States will be prepared to disengage selectively only designated portions, and immediately implement contingency measures to ensure the public's safety and continuity of commerce. This requires (1) a common framework with clearly defined roles for those charged with response and recovery; (2) ready forces that are properly trained and equipped to manage incidents, especially those involving WMD; (3) carefully crafted and exercised contingency plans for response, assessment, and recovery; and (4) extensive coordination among public, private, and international communities. As stated in the Maritime Transportation Security Act and the National Response Plan, the Department of Homeland Security, with the U.S. Coast Guard as its executive agency, has the primary responsibility for maritime homeland security, including the coordination of mitigation measures to expedite the recovery of infrastructure and transportation systems in the maritime domain, with the exception of DOD installations.

Although this Strategy advocates that incidents should be managed at the lowest possible organizational and jurisdictional level, maritime incidents of national significance will require the combined expertise of all levels of government and the private sector, and coordination with international trading partners. The United States will respond using the common coordinating structures contained within the National Response Plan and the National Incident Management System. Similarly, there is a need for corresponding international coordinating mechanisms to reconstitute commerce and minimize the global impact in the event of a significant maritime incident or threat.

The first line of response in the aftermath of any terrorist attack is the first-responder community – police officers, firefighters, emergency medical care providers, public works personnel, and emergency management officials. However, this first line of response may have only limited capabilities for dealing with the effects of a WMD event within the maritime domain, such as a nuclear or radiological dirty bomb exploded on a vessel in a major port area. The United States must build rapid-reaction forces to support first responders with capabilities to respond to WMD and other terrorist incidents that occur in the maritime domain. These response forces will blend the expertise and resources of the public and private sectors. They will be organized, trained, equipped, and exercised to operate in contaminated environments and manage the consequences of WMD incidents. Specifically, they will develop and deploy capabilities to detect and identify harmful chemical and biological agents, as well as conduct casualty extraction and mass decontamination in the maritime environment.

Concurrent with efforts to ensure the public's well-being, actions to maintain continuity of commerce must be implemented as quickly as possible, with a focus on expediting the recovery of maritime infrastructure, transportation systems, and affected maritime communities. Contingency and continuity plans for the public and private sector must be developed and exercised. Protocols for assessment, recovery, and reconstitution must effectively prioritize local, regional, and national interests, manage risk and uncertainty within acceptable levels, and achieve validation through regular drills and exercises. The marine transportation system will not be shut down as an automatic response to a maritime incident. Instead, a prudent and measured response will be taken based on an assessment of the specific incident, including available intelligence. Assessment and recovery efforts must be a shared responsibility of the public and private sectors. Accurate assessments regarding closures of selected commercial nodes within the marine transportation system, as well as effective efforts to redirect the affected modes of commerce, can only be achieved with the full cooperation of the private sector. To facilitate these actions, a formally recognized, national-level, coordinating body comprising private sector interests will liaison with Federal and State governments in developing and implementing these significant measures.

The direct and indirect costs associated with a prolonged and systemic disruption of the marine transportation system can be avoided by following the provisions of in-place contingency and continuity plans. These plans for assessment, recovery, and reconstitution must prioritize local, regional, and national interests, as well as manage risk and uncertainty within acceptable levels. These contingency and continuity plans must be developed and exercised in a coordinated fashion by the public and private sectors.

Section V
Conclusion

"Ultimately, the foundation of American strength is at home. It is in the skills of our people, the dynamism of our economy, and the resilience of our institutions. A diverse, modern society has inherent, ambitious, entrepreneurial energy. Our strength comes from what we do with that energy. That is where our national security begins."

National Security Strategy of the United States

This National Strategy presents a vision for the achievement of maritime security for the people and interests of the United States while respecting the information privacy and other legal rights of Americans. Moreover, it underscores our commitment to strengthening our international partnerships and advancing economic well-being around the globe by facilitating commerce and abiding by the principles of freedom of the seas.

As a vision for the future, it certainly faces some serious challenges. The sheer magnitude of the maritime domain complicates the arduous and complex task of maintaining maritime security. The United States confronts a diverse set of adversaries fully prepared to exploit this vast milieu for nefarious purposes. The seas serve as the medium for a variety of transnational threats that honor no national frontier and that seek to imperil the peace and prosperity of the world. Many of these threats mingle with legitimate commerce, either to provide concealment for carrying out hostile acts, or to make available weapons of mass destruction, their delivery systems, and related materials to nations and non-state actors of concern.

In this ambiguous security environment, responding to these unpredictable and transnational threats requires teamwork to prevent attacks, protect people and infrastructure, minimize damage, and expedite recovery. It necessitates the integration and alignment of all maritime security programs and initiatives into a far-reaching and unified national effort involving the Federal, State, local, and private sectors. Since September 11, 2001, Federal departments and agencies have risen uncompromisingly to the challenge of maritime security. But even an enhanced national effort is not sufficient. The challenges that remain ahead for the United States, the adversaries we confront, and the environment in which we operate compel us to strengthen our ties with allies and friends and to seek new partnerships with others. Therefore, international cooperation is critical to ensuring that lawful private and public activities in the maritime domain are protected from attack and hostile or unlawful exploitation. Such collaboration is fundamental to worldwide economic stability and growth, and it is vital to the interests of the United States. It is only through such an integrated approach among all maritime partners – governmental and nongovernmental, public and private – that we can improve the security of the maritime domain.

Thus, effective implementation of this National Strategy requires greater cooperation, not less. It requires deeper trust and confidence, not less. It requires a concerted application of collective capabilities to: increase our awareness of all activities and events in the maritime domain; enhance maritime security frameworks domestically and internationally; deploy a layered security based on law enforcement authorities, private sector partners' competencies, and military might; pursue transformational research and development to move to the next level of information fusion and analysis and WMD detection technologies for qualitative improvements in threat detection; and lastly improve our response posture should an incident occur.

With this National Strategy, the course has been set, but rhetoric is no substitute for action, and action is no substitute for success.

Annex A
Supporting Implementation Plans

This Strategy directs the coordination of United States Government maritime security programs and initiatives to achieve a comprehensive and cohesive national effort involving appropriate Federal, State, local, and private sector entities. In support of this Strategy, eight national implementation plans provide amplifying detail and specificity:

1. **National Plan to Achieve Maritime Domain Awareness** lays the foundation for an effective understanding of anything associated with the maritime domain that could impact the security, safety, economy, or environment of the United States, and identifying threats as early and as distant from our shores as possible.

2. **Global Maritime Intelligence Integration Plan** uses existing capabilities to integrate all available intelligence regarding potential threats to U.S. interests in the maritime domain.

3. **Maritime Operational Threat Response Plan** aims for coordinated United States Government response to threats against the United States and its interests in the maritime domain by establishing roles and responsibilities that enable the government to respond quickly and decisively.

4. **International Outreach and Coordination Strategy** provides a framework to coordinate all maritime security initiatives undertaken with foreign governments and international organizations, and solicits international support for enhanced maritime security.

5. **Maritime Infrastructure Recovery Plan** recommends procedures and standards for the recovery of the maritime infrastructure following attack or similar disruption.

6. **Maritime Transportation System Security Plan** responds to the President's call for recommendations to improve the national and international regulatory framework regarding the maritime domain.

7. **Maritime Commerce Security Plan** establishes a comprehensive plan to secure the maritime supply chain.

8. **Domestic Outreach Plan** engages non-Federal input to assist with the development and implementation of maritime security policies resulting from NSPD-41/HSPD-13.